Selling Liberty

Communicating Freedom in an Unfree World

Justin O'Donnell

2018

Updated 2022

Copyright © 2022 by Justin O'Donnell

All rights reserved. This book or any portion thereof may not be reproduced or used in any manner whatsoever without the express written permission of the publisher except for the use of brief quotations in a book review.

Printed in the United States of America

First Printing, 2018

Updated, 2022

ISBN-13: 978-1987568660

ISBN-10: 1987568664

TABLE OF CONTENTS

Selling Liberty — 7

Communicating Freedom in an Unfree World — 7

10 Steps to Having a Better Conversation — 15
- Step 1: Stop Talking and Listen — 18
- Step 2: Pay Attention, Fully — 20
- Step 3: Don't Preach — 22
- Step 4: Ask the Right Questions — 24
- Step 5: Don't get Sidetracked — 27
- Step 6: Know What You Don't Know — 29
- Step 7: You Already Said That — 31
- Step 8: The Details Don't Matter — 33
- Step 9: Your Experiences Aren't The Same — 35
- Step 10: Brevity — 37

Making an impact — 40
- Phase 1: Initiate the Conversation — 43
- Phase 2: Make a Friend — 45
- Phase 3: Proactive Discovery — 48
- Phase 4: Advice and Consent — 51
- Phase 5: Take It Home — 53

Controlling the Conversation — 59
- Using Words with Power — 61
- Two-Step Apologies — 63
- Opportunity 1: Introducing Yourself — 66
- Opportunity 2: Telling a Story — 69

Copyright © 2022 Justin O'Donnell

Opportunity 3: Giving Your Presentation — 71
Opportunity 4: Closing Statements — 74
Opportunity 5: The Follow-Up — 76

The 5 Traits of a Salesman — 80
Trait 1: Positivity — 82
Trait 2: Eagerness To Learn — 84
Trait 3: Grind and Hustle — 86
Step 4: Be Professional — 88
Step 5: Be Hungry — 90

The 7 Skills of Success — 92
Skill 1: Be Curious — 94
Skill 2: Empathize — 96
Skill 3: Don't Make Assumptions — 99
Skill 4: Read Between the Lines — 101
Skill 5: Assume Good Intent — 104
Skill 6: Be The Expert — 106
Skill 7: Know What You Don't Know — 108

12 Keys to Winning and Losing Debates — 111
Step 1: Stay Calm — 113
Step 2: Back It Up — 115
Step 3: Ask Questions — 117
Step 4: Connect The Dots — 119
Step 5: Take The High Ground — 121
Step 6: Keep Listening — 123
Step 7: Give Them Credit — 125
Step 8: Do Your Homework — 127
Step 9: Move the Needle — 129
Step 10: Stick to the Issues — 131
Step 11: Don't Get Distracted — 133

Copyright © 2022 Justin O'Donnell

Step 12: Know Your Strengths   134

Tuning Your Marketing   **137**
    Step 1: Identify Your Target Audience   141
    Step 2: Identify Their Problems   143
    Step 3: Offer Help   145
    Step 4: Reference Success   147
    Step 5: How Are You Different?   149
    The Messaging Mistake   151
    Now Put It All Together   153

Moving the Overton Window   **155**
    The Axis of Freedom   157
    Moving the Needle   159
    Engaging in New Media   162

Why do I Care   **164**
    Why I'm a Libertarian - an Essay   165
    What Motivates You?   171

Copyright © 2022 Justin O'Donnell

Copyright © 2022 Justin O'Donnell

SELLING LIBERTY

COMMUNICATING FREEDOM IN AN UNFREE WORLD

In my journey with the Libertarian Party, a few things have become abundantly clear. One of the most obvious is the passion of our activists and volunteers. These are people dedicated beyond reasonable expectations towards realizing a world made freer by their efforts. Never before have I encountered an organization whose members were so willing to entertain personal and financial sacrifice as such a normal requisite of their commitment to a political cause. I've seen petitioners standing for hours in the rain fighting for ballot access. I have seen people use all of their workplace sick time to attend political rallies and protests. I have seen people travel hundreds of miles at a moment's notice to help a candidate in another state deliver materials. I have seen people willingly uproot their entire lives and families to move to New Hampshire in the hopes of helping the Free State Project build a functional Libertarian Diaspora in the North East.

And through all of this, I have also seen a persistent trend of failure in these, our most honestly dedicated volunteers. When it comes to spreading the message of Liberty beyond our echo chamber, beyond the ears already willing to hear what we have to say - we don't stand up to the measure of the game. At every Libertarian convention, I attend I do my best to meet as many new people as possible, and while a few have definitely stood out above the rest as having an innate ability to communicate, most have not. I see a trend among those I meet in Libertarian circles. And the trend ties very closely to career and education.

Our movement is inherently intellectual. Liberty is a philosophy grounded in intellect and logic, rather than emotion and empathy. Those that appear to be naturally attracted to our philosophical underpinnings are typically closely aligned to particular career fields. More often than not when I meet new people at Libertarian conventions and events and ask them what they do, the majority will tell me they are software engineers, or researchers, or have several advanced degrees in economics or other technical fields. What lacks is activists whose field of expertise is marketing, sales, teaching, or other fields that require empathy, and constant personal interaction. While we have many people who know the ins and outs of liberty and our philosophy, we have very few people who can sell that message to those who wouldn't have arrived at the logical conclusions on their own. And that is a problem that we can fix.

Now, this observation is not universal, but it is also not unique. Routinely we hear pundits and detractors refer to libertarians as a bunch of autistic folks stuck behind their keyboards. The obvious invalidity of the insult aside, why is this perception what is so inherently assumed about us? Well, all those amazing activists I mentioned who do great and beautiful things, go unnoticed because most of them are not salespeople. They don't leave lingering perceptions in the minds of those they speak to. They generally present their arguments and strongly lay out our platform and goals, get their signatures and move on. Have they been effective? Yes. Have they been memorable? No.

Unlike most Libertarian activists, my background is actually in sales. I have made my living talking to people, and leaving a good enough impression that not only do they remember me, but call me back and trust me enough to actually buy my product. The mindset, the skills, and the communication style I have learned from a career in sales have led me to a different kind of success within the libertarian party. When petitioning for Ballot Access for Gary Johnson, I was averaging several Hundred signatures a day higher than any of my colleagues in New England. When tabling at events, I have had greater success getting people to actually stick around and have a conversation rather than simply taking literature and moving on. When it comes to the effort of herding cats that is leading a libertarian organization, I found myself serving as a Regional Representative to the libertarian National Committee a mere two years after first joining the party. Is my experience truly unique? Is it a natural gift? Not at all.

I found myself working in sales quite by accident, as I'm sure many people do. I was unhappy with a job I had that was in the field of my education and built on my experience in the United States Army, and when I was offered a Job in a sales position, I jumped at it without doing my full due diligence as an escape from what I considered mundane. Now, taking that job turned out to be one of the biggest mistakes, and best moves I ever made in my life. The company I went to work for was nothing more than an outside sales organization selling poorly priced Life Insurance products and structured as a multi-level marketing scheme- but what I learned and carried away changed my life forever.

I grew up as the picture of introversion, highly intelligent, bored with school yet still managed straight A's in honors classes, and skated through college without even trying. By the time I joined the Army, I was the personal picture of what I described as our communications problems. I was on track to being an engineer and relied on my smarts to get me through Life. That wasn't going to fly when trying to sell people something they didn't need and didn't want, and working purely on commission. I had to adapt, I had to change the way I spoke, the way I listened, and the way I communicated on every level. Years later, here I am making a living by teaching others how to do what I was forced into by bad luck and impulse.

The point I'm getting across here is that inside us all is a salesman, and I'm not talking about a fancy snake oil salesman who uses flash and glamour to con people into buying what he has. Inside all of us there is a true honest salesman, who believes in what they are doing, and truly wants to help people understand what they are selling. The first step to realizing your inner selling power is to realize how much of it you've already been using in your everyday life and career. Ask yourself, as a software engineer, how often is it that you have to justify to someone else why you chose a particular solution to a problem when there was more than one option - you sold it. In any field of work, you will eventually have to justify the reasons behind your actions, and that is when your most basic sales skills instinctively come into play.

What I aim to do isn't teach anyone how to reinvent the wheel, and surely I don't want to change your personality or what makes you unique. What I will express here are simply some fundamental principles and skills I have learned and taught over the years that can help to improve how we have conversations, how we debate, how we argue, how we listen, and how we sell. These are not skills that only have use in sales either, in fact, some of them can universally apply to our everyday conversations.

There are only a few main topics that we will cover. If you can master even only one of these topics, you should see an improvement in your communications with political adversaries, friends, and family alike. In the following chapters, I'm going to teach you the Rules for having a better Conversation, how to Make an Impact, Some tricks to Controlling The Dialogue, How to Win and Lose a Debate, the Traits of Salespeople, The Skills of Success, and the importance of tuning your marketing.

As we progress through this book, pay attention and take notes. Make notes in the margins, earmark pages that pique your interest, and most importantly, put what you learn into practice. And when we're done, be prepared to have better conversations, better presentations, and better results in your daily interactions.

10 Steps to Having a Better Conversation

One of the hardest things we do in everyday life is simply having conversations. Sure we talk to plenty of people as we go about our business, but in the age of automation, that is becoming easier to avoid, and many of us go out of our way to use the self-checkout to avoid having to talk to another human being. Escaping conversations isn't the true issue at hand, but rather our inability to have those conversations when we want to, never mind when we need to. Without the ability to have a conversation we can't effectively communicate our ideas, and without that, our battle is lost. Many of us believe that this issue is not something we need to work on. We've worked outreach booths, done petition drives, canvased and door-knocked for candidates- surely we've become comfortable talking to people, right?

Well, that is just the problem. Talking to people is the skill of a teacher, not of a salesman. We aren't doing these things just to check off the list and move on to the next task, if we're going to grow the movement and succeed at our tasks, then we must first learn to stop talking to people, and start having conversations with them instead. What we're going to discuss here is the ability to have a conversation, and some tips and tricks to make conversations better. These skills are not inherently specific to the nature of political activism, and I encourage people to put them into practice in their personal lives as well.

While Facebook, texting, and other technologies provide us immense opportunities to have impersonal communication, there is nothing more powerful than the face to face conversation as a tool to connect to someone. Whether that someone is a voter, a volunteer, or a friend or colleague, the importance of communicating your ideas, and listening to theirs is important. Building rapport and having these conversations is one of the fundamental cores of success in business and life. With these skills, you'll be able to converse confidently and freely while maintaining control of the conversations you have.

Step 1: Stop Talking and Listen

The first step in improving your conversational skills is quite simply the easiest. Stop talking. While this may be the easiest to grasp, it may honestly be the hardest to put into practice. It is a very basic human instinct to want to control a conversation, and many of us fall into the trap of believing that if we are talking, then we are in control. When we are talking we aren't listening, we may be controlling the flow of the conversation, but we have no idea of its impact. It is crucial that more than we talk, we listen, and not just hear, but listen.

Buddha said *"A dog is not considered a good dog because he is a good barker. A man is not considered a good man because he is a good talker."* This gets to the core of conversational skills. And think about it from a personal experience, we've all been in situations where we couldn't get a word in edgewise, and felt unfulfilled by the conversations we were having. By speaking as little as possible, and actively and intently listening to those we speak to, we can have a more profound impact on the conversation when we do choose to speak.

Something that is often overlooked and forgotten when it comes to listening skills, is the reason why we are listening. We don't want to get into the trap of listening with the intent of responding. We aren't in this to simply win an argument. The reason we need to listen to those we converse with is to understand them. When we listen to understand we don't just hear what they said, but why they think that. When we do respond, we can do so from a position of understanding and empathy, as opposed to combative debate tactics. Once we reach a level of understanding and can empathize with the points being made to us, we can craft a response that respects those feelings and encourages informed thought - which ultimately, is the goal of any conversation.

Step 2: Pay Attention, Fully

Everyone knows what it's like to try and talk to someone while they're checking their texts and Facebook notifications on their phones. Multi-tasking not only distracts from the conversations at hand but in some cases, it is downright disrespectful. If you're going to have a conversation with someone, have a conversation with them. Don't allow yourself to be distracted by everything else that's not happening at that moment. Don't worry, Facebook will be there when you're done.

But it isn't just our phones and electronics that distract us, to be honest, it's our lives. When someone is speaking to you, not only put down the phone but focus on the person you are with, not on the argument you had with your boss. It doesn't matter what you're going to have for dinner, and it sure as hell doesn't matter whether someone just liked your most recent Instagram post.

You're engaged in a conversation for a reason, so commit to it, and be a part of it. Be present in the circumstance, and dedicate yourself to the task at hand. If you don't want to be in that conversation, that's ok, you can leave it. By all means, find an opportunity and leave the conversation, excuse yourself for something that's inherently more important. But definitely, do not be half there. Engaging in a conversation is a task in and of itself.

We have all been guilty of this, myself included. But give it a try and you'll realize how much more you'll enjoy the people you have conversations with when you allow yourself to fully listen to them, without the distractions and mindless scrolling through your news feed. Because a conversation at its heart requires more than just giving someone your attention, but giving them your *undivided* attention, and participating fully.

Step 3: Don't Preach

A conversation isn't the place for your soliloquy. Another of the most common mistakes made when having a conversation is the tendency to pontificate endlessly without any opportunity for interjection. Worse even than not being listened to, is being talked at. Lecturing someone is not having a conversation, but rather reinforcing your desire to hear yourself talk.

Sometimes we need to vent, sometimes there's something you just need to get off your chest, and you don't quite care what the other person has to say about it. In that case, let's not confuse ourselves into believing that we're having a conversation because we are far from it. There's nothing inherently wrong with utilizing this style of communication, so long as it's not our primary conversational style. Preaching is generally hostile and combative, regardless of the intent of the speaker.

Nobody wants to be spoken to and preached to without the possibility of coming to healthy points and exchanges of ideas. Sometimes we need to set aside our personal opinions to enter each conversation assuming that we have something to learn. We should expect to give opportunities for pushback in responses and arguments, or else we stifle the ability of the conversation to teach us anything and limit our own ability to grow. If those aren't things you can accept, then don't have a conversation about it, go and write a blog instead.

Copyright © 2022 Justin O'Donnell

Step 4: Ask the Right Questions

How many times have you been working an outreach booth, knocking on doors while canvassing, or tried talking to customers, and been roadblocked by yes and no one-word answers? When I first started it was the most frustrating thing I dealt with. You've made fantastic points, and you drove your message hard, so how come the prospect replies with a universal conversation killer? The one-word response?

Simple, your questions were too complicated. When you present someone with a complicated situation, they are going to give you the simplest answer they can. And while that may very well have answered your question, it didn't give you anything to follow up with to keep the conversation going any longer. Open-ended questions allow you to get the person you are speaking with to provide you with information that will help you guide the conversation and enjoy your time with it.

 This skill does inherently build on the previously discussed skills of listening rather than talking, and avoiding your tendency to preach, but it will fundamentally change how people will talk to you, based on what you ask them. When we look at this from a perspective of political outreach, or even sales, the idea is that you don't want to tell the prospect why you're right, you want to get them to come to that conclusion on their own by following a logical progression. We can do this by building on what was previously said and asking simple questions that get complex answers. Ask them "What was it Like?" or "How did it feel?" and let them describe to you the situation, rather than explaining it to them.

 When someone is guided rather than taught, then the inevitable conclusion is self-realization rather than a confrontation. Yes, we want to challenge their ideals and preconceptions, but before they can embrace ours, they must first question their own. The most control you will ever have in a conversation is when you ask a simple question, and the other person has to pause to think about how to respond to it. While they are busy thinking about how to answer you, they are questioning whether or not their opinion holds. And let's be honest, it will be far more interesting of a response than a simple "yes" or "no" that gives you nothing to build on.

Copyright © 2022 Justin O'Donnell

Step 5: Don't get Sidetracked

We've all been there sitting with a friend and having a great conversation and then we remember something funny that happened last week and we just have to share it. Don't. It doesn't matter how great or interesting your story is, don't interrupt someone else. And even worse, when someone else is speaking, don't wait around impatiently for them to finish just so you can change the subject.

An interjection isn't a bad thing in its own right. You can interject if you're short, don't derail the speaker, and help reinforce the point of the person talking. But don't forget to listen, and give others the space to tell their story. But when we move a conversation off track to relate our anecdote, without responding to what was said, it signals to others that we either weren't listening or didn't care about what they had to say. When you lose the trust of the person you are talking to, you have lost the conversation and are no longer on equal footing.

    Focus on what's being said, and when thoughts come into your mind, let them just as freely leave your mind. Remember, we are listening not to respond, but to understand. And if we focus on our contribution, then we can't fully understand the points of others.

Step 6: Know What You Don't Know

If a conversation is exceeding your knowledge base, then don't pretend to be the expert. Acknowledge the limits of your expertise and relinquish the question to further investigation. There is nothing worse than losing your credibility because you try to bluff your way through an argument of fact. However, an admission of not knowing is often more endearing than having the right answer off-hand.

There is an anecdote from my time in the Army that always stuck with me in this matter. A young soldier was going before a promotion board where he was to be drilled relentlessly with all manner of questions regarding military history, customs and traditions, and job-based knowledge. While preparing and studying for this board, our seniors drilled into us that confidence was more important than being right and that if you were unsure, just answer with confidence even if you were wrong. However, one soldier didn't do that. He paused, faltered, and then answered *"I apologize sir, but I do not know the answer at this time, however, I shall research it and return with the answer as soon as possible."* Later that day when those officers were leaving the boardroom, that young soldier was waiting, for the answer to the question he didn't know previously. He was promoted that month and I wasn't.

Honesty will always be your best policy when dealing with difficult situations. If you don't know something, simply say that you don't know it. Being caught in a lie will destroy the trust, and the cohesion of the conversation you are trying to have. And when you are trying to convince someone to join your cause, the last thing you want is to look stupid.

Step 7: You Already Said That

Repetition is great for memorization, but it kills a conversation. Frankly, it's boring. Repeating a point you've already made gives the impression that you aren't focused on the shared aspect of the conversation, and simply want to drive your point home as deep as possible. Seriously, how self-centered do you have to be to forget what *you* already said?

It doesn't matter how many times you rephrase it, if you're making the same point, they get that, and will generally feel as if you're talking down to them after hearing it so many times. A conversation is a back-and-forth, exchange, and evolution of ideas. When you constantly repeat yourself, you aren't having a conversation anymore but are setting yourself up to argue. And no matter what you think on Facebook threads, no one ever wins an argument.

Often people ask why repetition is so harmful to conversations. And while I'm no child psychologist, I have noticed a trend in parenting where we will use repetition to teach and train children on proper conduct and to temper their actions. Perhaps, there is something to the notion that constantly repeating yourself has a negative connotation where people feel they are being talked down to as a child would be. But just because you feel that you have a point to make, that doesn't necessarily mean repetition is the right way to make it.

Step 8: The Details Don't Matter

Do you know all those minute details you drag up to draw out your point and make it more impactful? Well, in reality, no one cares about them. When you're having a conversation with someone, what they are interested in is you and what you have to say.

When you spend too much time qualifying the points you've made by spouting what amounts to trivia, the point itself is lost in the drivel. Now, this isn't to say that you shouldn't include any facts to support your argument, but you need to know which ones suit the conversation, and which ones are just there to prove that you're the smartest person in the room, which by the way, you aren't.

So remember this when you're about to spout that name, date, or other trivial detail where it might not be needed. Adding details to a conversation is only worthwhile if they serve to better the understanding of your listener, as opposed to your peace of mind. Be succinct, be clear, be thorough, but never over-educate.

Step 9: Your Experiences Aren't The Same

People complain, it's what they do. Whenever you're talking to someone, whether having a serious conversation or just a passing quip, there is a chance that there is something they have to complain about. Now, sometimes the complaints are just for the sake of complaining, but usually, they'll relate an experience that left a negative impact on them.

I'm going to be extraordinarily blunt on this one. Their experience is different than yours, and nothing that has happened to you is equal to or the same as what happened to them. When they talk about having a bad day at work, you do not tell them how much you hate your job. If they just lost a family member, do not talk about a recent loss of your own.

By equating their experiences with your own, you are not building rapport or finding common ground. Quite the opposite, you are minimizing their experiences and denying them the importance of their individual experiences. There are many ways to use conversation to build rapport, and this is quite possibly one of the most dismissive and hurtful attempts at it possible. Even when you experience an event with someone, and it's a shared experience, the impact of that experience can vary greatly between individuals. So what's most important to remember here when it comes to conversational impact - it's not about you.

Step 10: Brevity

Of all the steps I've mentioned so far, this one may be the most important. Keep things short, brief, concise, and to the point. A great conversation doesn't drone on. You can say a lot in a brief time, especially if you listen and understand where others are coming from. If you drag it out too long, interest will fade, and the opportunity presented will be wasted. Leave people with your ideas fresh in their heads, and not overwhelmed. If you've conveyed your points accurately and appropriately, you will get another shot, at another conversation, when they come back to you. Know when it's appropriate to end the conversation.

A good conversation is like a mini-skirt, long enough to cover the subject, but short enough to hold your attention.

Now What?

So far we've discussed 10 steps to improve a single aspect of our outreach, our conversational skills. We went over a lot, and these aren't the easiest changes to make. But they aren't just applicable in political outreach. These steps can help improve the conversations you have in your everyday life.

Now, what I want you to do now is pick one of these steps. It doesn't matter which one, and make that change right away. And when you see an improvement in your everyday conversational enjoyment, start adding pieces to the puzzle. Now we aren't done by a long shot, we haven't discussed sales tactics or how to sell your ideas, but the ability to have a conversation is paramount before you can start directing the nature and content of those conversations.

Start with your family dinner, put the phones away, and listen to each other. Understand how everyone felt about their day. Avoid changing the subject. And avoid hostile and controlling communication styles.

But above all, enjoy the conversations you're having.

Copyright © 2022 Justin O'Donnell

MAKING AN IMPACT

When you're having better conversations, you are one step closer to accomplishing your goal with each and every attempt. What is that goal you might ask? The ultimate goal is to make an impact on those you speak with. Making an impact may take shape in a number of different ways. Whether you convince someone to buy what you're selling, consider your point of view, change their mind about something, or just remember a pleasant conversation, you've had an impact on them. Whether you impacted their day or even their life, you've had an impact on them. The goal in sales is to impact their decision, and the goal in politics is to impact their views. What doesn't change, is the need to make an impact.

Making an impact means you'll be remembered, and in effect, you've changed the course of events for the person you're interacting with. So how can we make the best of each opportunity, and give ourselves the most opportunity with each conversation? How do we make sure that our conversations will be meaningful enough to have that lasting impact we're looking for?

Every salesperson has a process, and that sales process is the key to closing their deals. Whether they have a script, a questionnaire, a slide deck, or a pitch, they have a process and they stick to it like religious gospel. They stick to it for a reason, because it works. They've developed and honed that process over the course of their career, and it works for them and their clientele. Whether they developed it themselves or were taught by a mentor, their particular words may change, but the structure of their process never deviates.

In this section, we're going to discuss one such process, why it works, and how to implement it to its fullest potential. Building on our previous work in improving our skills as conversationalists, we're going to take the next step and make sure that our conversations have an Impact. Our process isn't simple, but it is structured. I don't believe in scripts, because no two people are the same, and how they respond to your inquiries will differ. This 5-phase process is simply called IMPACT.

1. **I**nitiate The Conversation
2. **M**ake a Friend
3. **P**roactive Discovery
4. **A**dvice and **C**onsent
5. **T**ake it Home

Those 5 steps are how we're going to make a lasting IMPACT on those we're selling. The name is catchy too, don't mind the repetition, it was a build-up.

Phase 1: Initiate the Conversation

Every time you say hello, smile, greet a stranger or ask a question, you've initiated a conversation. But it's not enough to simply say the words and kick things off. We initiate hundreds of conversations a week, and we rarely give them a second thought. The checkout girl at the grocery store, the customer service rep at your cable company, the teller at the bank - you initiated conversations with each of these people just in the course of going through your daily routine. But, did you make an IMPACT on any of them?

In order to make an impact, the first step isn't merely starting any old conversation, but initiating a conversation with intent and invitation. The opening of each conversation is one of the driving factors in determining the tone and result of what follows. A melancholy opening, unconfident and quiet, will convey to a prospect that you are just that - unconfident, as well as unenthusiastic. If you can't muster the enthusiasm to be excited about your own pitch, then why should anyone be excited to hear it from you? When you're in control of a conversation, your tone and excitement can bring the other person up to your level. A previously apathetic passerby can be turned into a willing prospect with something as simple as a cheerful hello, and a confident invitation to talk.

So be loud, be excited, and be enthusiastic with your hellos. Butt don't be overwhelming and go so far that you scare someone away. By setting a friendly and welcoming tone with your invitation and opening, you set the stage for the conversation, and the chance to make your pitch. Because only with a great opening, can you have the chance to turn a sour prospect, into a friend.

Phase 2: Make a Friend

No matter what sales process someone uses, everyone understands the importance of building rapport with their prospects and clients. We don't need to take long to explain what rapport is, its dictionary definition does well enough - **"a close and harmonious relationship in which the people or groups concerned understand each other's feelings or ideas and communicate well."** That sounds kind of like a friend, doesn't it?

Making a friend of a prospect doesn't mean you're gonna have to hang out with them, don't worry. But it does mean that you're going to have to get to know them, at least a little bit. It's important to know what makes them tick, how they think, and where they're coming from in relation to where you want them to be at the end of the pitch. And before any prospect is gonna listen to what you have to say, never mind buy your product, you have to convince them to trust you.

Trust is the operative word here, and it's something we'll repeat ad nauseam throughout this book. There are a few tips and tricks to getting someone to like you, trust you, and at least for the moment consider you a friend. With almost anyone on earth, you can find something in common, some common ground from which to build the foundation of your friendship, no matter how brief. Common wisdom says to avoid religion and politics as you embark on this endeavor, but since one of our goals here is ultimately political, we'll consider that as a starting point to work from.

When trying to find common ground with a political prospect, perhaps with the intent of turning them into a likely voter or supporter, start by asking them sincerely what issues matter to them, and what views they hold. Even if only one position is shared, that is more than enough to begin exploring other facets of the product being sold. The key here is to focus on finding something to agree on, rather than persuading them to your perspective, and to help the prospect view you as someone trustworthy and worth listening to.

Phase 3: Proactive Discovery

Proactive discovery is the process by which you can use questions in the form of a conversation to learn information about the person you're talking to and what really matters to them. Every person has needs and wants, and usually, their wants are informed by their needs. Many people may not really know what they need when they're expressing their wants, and in reality, find themselves ignorant of their needs. When they confuse the two and misrepresent their wants for needs, it is incumbent upon you to determine what the actual needs of the individual are.

The need beneath the need is one of the most important pieces of information you can gather from a conversation with a prospect. When someone tells you what they want, and is presenting it in a manner of something they need, they may be providing you with limited information through no fault of their own.

It's up to you to identify the need beneath the need, and what the real underlying issues are that are causing the problems they're trying to address. In most circumstances people will ask you to treat the symptoms that are bothering them, unaware of the underlying disease that is causing the discomfort. Simply going based on the presented information without delving for clarification wouldn't make you a very good doctor.

The metaphor of a symptom versus the disease is fitting, even if not entirely accurate when it comes to sales and political persuasion. When you are selling someone something, you're trying to solve a problem for them - a problem they might not even know they have. When it comes to politics, the same principles apply. Each of your political positions is designed to address some issue facing society, and how those issues affect individuals will vary from one person to another. When someone tells you their complaints, it is prudent to ask probing questions to find the source of what's bothering them, because often it will be deeper than even they realize. Solving the need beneath their need, satisfies a customer for life, while simply treating a symptom will allow the disease to fester and re-emerge at a later time.

Phase 4: Advice and Consent

Once you've established the true needs of your prospect, the goal of this sales process isn't to bully your way into a sale or to lie to your prospects to convince them to buy what you're selling. You aren't a sleazy used car salesman, or a harlot peddling snake oil, you're trying to establish yourself as credible and trustworthy, so your pitch makes a lasting impact on your prospect. The key isn't just to get them to buy what you're selling but to convince them that they actually want and need it and that there's a good reason that they're buying it.

Instead of playing the part of a salesman, consider yourself to be filling the role of an advisor. While your goal might be to get someone to buy what you're selling, the path you're taking to accomplish that is not a high-pressure push. As an advisor, you're charged with giving the prospect all the relevant information, and educating them on the scope of the problem as you understand it. If you were able to identify their need beneath the need, then help them realize it as well. Once the problems are known, and the prospect is aware of their scope and understands your perspective in trying to solve the issue, you can present them with options on how to address the issues. In the end, you aren't asking them to buy anything, but simply offering them the opportunity to solve their problem.

When you present your sale as a recommendation from an advisor, the ultimate decision the prospect has to make isn't whether or not to buy what you're selling, but whether or not to take steps to solve their problems. When they arrive at the decision on their own, their commitment is significantly stronger than if they were told what to do and what to think. The key to providing advice is to secure consent, as the prospect fully buys into what you've guided them to understand. From this position, the sale closes itself, as the prospect has convinced themselves, based on the guidance you've provided.

Phase 5: Take It Home

Now that your prospect is ready to buy, it's time to close the deal. Whether you're selling insurance or solar installation, fundraising for a non-profit, or campaigning for election, the close is the most important part of every interaction and sales pitch. This is your last chance to reaffirm the decision your prospect has made and to confirm their commitment. This is the last chance you'll have to probe for uneasiness and hesitation from the buyer. It may seem counterintuitive, but the goal of your close isn't necessarily just to secure the sale, but it's to give the prospect the final opportunity to say no. And you want them to say no.

Your closing process should be structured to meticulously and repeatedly ask for buy-in and confirmation of intent. You should ask plenty of questions to elicit an affirmative response and pay attention to any hesitation in the answers. A yes is a yes, a maybe, sure, ok, or I guess, are all no's. You want to make sure that the prospect is as confident in their decision to buy, as you were in your pitch and proposition to sell. And if you aren't confident enough to ask them for a solid commitment, then you know deep down that your pitch was weak. You would much rather find out now that they aren't committed, than have to deal with a return or failure to follow through on payment after the fact. And a satisfied customer is a potential repeat customer. And a happy repeat customer can bring you the greatest gift a salesperson can ask for - a referral and a recruit.

When considering applying the IMPACT sales process to political persuasion, your close is going to be a unique experience. Politics isn't something solved on the fly, and political opinions don't change overnight. Usually, people's political opinions are formed based on a lifetime of experiences, their personal ethics, and the moral codes and structures they adhere to. To change someone's mind about something that is so fundamentally part of their personality and identity takes time. The close of a political sale is going to be a perpetually ongoing experience, constantly reaffirming the former prospect, and now supporter, that they made the right choice. Maintaining their support requires contact and involvement, so keep that in mind.

Copyright © 2022 Justin O'Donnell

What Next?

So now that we've talked about how to improve our basic conversational skills, and how to use them to have an impact on those we talk to, we should put them into practice as often as possible. If you're not working in sales, or not currently on a campaign, and unsure of where and when it would be appropriate to practice, don't worry. You can again, use these skills to make an impact not just on prospective clients, customers, recruits, and converts, but on people in your everyday life. This sales process isn't exclusive to interactions where something is being bought or sold.

You may have caught yourself thinking about how the 10 Skills to Have a Better Conversation we discussed in the previous chapter would very seamlessly apply to these steps of the Impact sales process. This would be true of almost any sales process, because the reality is, that all that a sale is, is a conversation with a transaction of value involved at its conclusion. Much like how the 10 steps can apply to any everyday conversation, so would the impact sales process if you choose to apply it.

Why would you want to apply a sales process to everyday conversations? Simple, because according to some philosophies, every interaction you have with another person is already transactional in nature. In each conversation you have, there is a sale that happens. Whether or not you realize it, every interaction involved the exchange of ideas and the exchange of trust. With every point made, and every objection heard, a pitch and a sale are made. If you've ever worked in direct sales, consider the fact that every pitch you ever gave resulted in a sale - Either you sold something to your customer, or they sold you an excuse of why they wouldn't buy it. But in the end, someone was sold, it just may have been you.

So consider how you could apply this process in your life at work when communicating with teammates, bosses, and hopefully your clients and customers. Exercise the intent to make an impact not just on your sales calls, but on every conversation you have. And once you master having better conversations, and structuring their process with a purpose, you can begin the journey to exercising control of those conversations.

Controlling the Conversation

Now that we've gone over how to structure our sales process and have the best conversation we can, the next lesson should be on how to control that conversation, in tone and direction. Simply having a balance conversation is meaningful in your daily life, but in order to use those skills in business, sales or politics, you need to know how to take control of those situations. When you're able to take control of these conversations, you'll be able to guide those you speak with to come to the conclusions you want.

One of the first steps in controlling any conversation is the establishment of trust. There's an old adage in sales, that the only true objection is trust.

If someone doesn't trust you, then why would they buy something from you? The same is going to hold true with your activism. If you can't earn someone's trust, then what makes you think that you can earn their support?

There are a number of tactics that successful salespeople use to build trust in relationships with new clients, and there is simply no way we could cover them all. What we are going to focus on are a few methods that I have found easily translated from sales and consulting over to outreach and politics. First, we are going to cover a few more tips for improving a sales-based conversation, specific to controlling it.

Using Words with Power

Your vocabulary is one of your biggest strengths and biggest weaknesses at the same time. And while we never discussed altering your vocabulary to improve your conversational skills, now is the time to focus on a few tricks to change some things up. Something we naturally do when having conversations is separate from each other and focus on our distinctions. It makes us proud to be unique, deep down we all want to be special, and we are always distrustful of someone trying to sell us something.

When building trust with prospects, how we talk to them is incredibly important. In sales and politics alike, you'll very rarely be talking to someone who doesn't have a problem. The intent when starting a conversation is to find that problem as soon as possible. We can do this by building trust with language. The word "we" is your new most powerful weapon.

While we still want to avoid equating experiences, we want to focus on collectivizing actions. When people are convinced that we are in it with them, and going through the process beside them, they are more likely to trust us. Going through the conversation as part of a group will endear a sense of companionship to those you speak to.

This change is simple, yet incredibly effective. If you don't believe me, just reread the last few paragraphs we went over. We can use these subtle changes to change how our words are perceived, build trust and take control. Once we've established trust with the person we're speaking to, then they'll finally tell us what the problem is, making our proactive discovery phase infinitely easier and less combative. In sales, this is where you figure out how your product can solve their problem, but in politics, this is where we tie their problems into our solutions.

Two-Step Apologies

When we're finally made aware of the problem, there's a trick to use called the two-step apology. In these circumstances, we can hope that we are never actually the cause of their problems, but we apologize to further our rapport and show empathy. But the second step in that apology is what builds towards our direction, where we assert our newfound control and steer the conversation in the direction we want to go.

For example, let's look toward a real-life example from the world of health insurance sales. Whenever I got a call from a prospective client, they always had a problem and were looking for help in fixing it. When I finally had a grasp of the problem, I responded with the same exact line every single time.

"I'm sorry that's happening to you, but let's see what we can do to solve that problem today. We're

going to go over the problem and the current policy, while exploring the other options available to us. When we find a new policy that solves this problem, we'll go ahead and get it set up as soon as possible to handle this problem. How does that sound to you?"

With that one statement, I took complete control of the mission and direction of our conversation.

But let's dissect that sentence just a bit more. I opened with an apology to show empathy and endear them to me. I followed that by laying out a plan of action as the second step of the two-step apology. And all throughout it, I used the collective words to reinforce that we were in it together and that they had a partner to help them figure it out as opposed to a salesman trying to sling a product. The ending here might be the most important part though. I assured them that a solution would be found and that we would take care of it today, and asked them how they felt about it.

That last sentence is what we call a 'trial close.' The trial close gives us one of two possibilities going forward. At that moment the prospect is going to tell you that they want to move forward and handle it today, or they'll stop you and let you know they aren't ready to make a decision today. Either way, you've gotten them to buy into the idea and trust you enough to move forward with your conversation. This helps set the expectations that we're moving towards a solution, and that it involves a commitment from them to do so.

At this point, we've already taken complete control of our conversation, built a foundation of trust and set the tone, direction, and expectations for where we want it to go. All of this in the first few moments of speaking to our prospect.

Now, with an understanding of group comfort language, two-step apologies, and trial closes, we're ready to break down the structure of a controlled conversation. Every conversation is a sale, and this is where we're going to start breaking down the steps to controlling our sales process. As before, we're going to do this by breaking down the conversation into five key opportunities to control a conversation.

Opportunity 1: Introducing Yourself

One thing that sets apart conversations with friends and family from those with prospects or clients is the introduction. With friends and family, you likely don't need to introduce yourself, but this step can still be useful. The introduction is where you establish yourself, and set the tone for the conversation. What we've discussed about the use of language and the two-step apology takes place in this step of the conversation.

Introducing yourself is about more than just sharing your name, it's about letting the other person know who they're speaking to. Your credibility and expertise are what need to be established. When you are introducing yourself to someone, you should make sure to subtly highlight what sets you apart from others they may talk to. Are you licensed in your field?

Are you a leader in your county or state party? Lead with that. People respect credentials, even if it's something you don't think highly of. By establishing your credibility while building initial trust during the introductory phase, you establish your place of authority in the conversation.

But aside from dominance and establishing control, there are a few more tricks to making the introduction go smoothly. Make sure that you smile when starting a new conversation. Regardless of how you feel or what's going on, displaying a smile makes you more approachable to people you interact with. A frown is unfriendly, and an unfriendly face is often enough to turn away a potential prospect.

Remember to always maintain eye contact when having a conversation with someone. This may be difficult when speaking to groups, but it's important to always be looking someone in the eyes. When you maintain eye contact during conversation, you display outward confidence and reinforce the trust you've previously built. People are much more apt to listen to what you have to say if you're looking them in the eyes when you say it. The final thing to remember here is to be enthusiastic. Excitement is contagious, and if you are excited about what you are talking about, then the people you are talking to will be excited to hear about it. Be excited to get people excited about listening.

Opportunity 2: Telling a Story

Everyone likes a good story, a tale woven to impart a lesson or send a message even more so. The story you tell is what creates a connection beyond the introduction. Your story is an explanation of what you are representing and the message you are promoting. The best part of telling a story is its ability to captivate an audience. But in order to maintain that attention, you must remember the importance of brevity. The best stories are short and brief. They get to the point and don't go off the rails. If your story is too long, then you run the risk of people losing interest and ceasing to care what you have to say anymore.

The purpose of your story should be to build curiosity. If done right it will get people excited about what you have to offer, and ideally, they'll want to know more. But here's the key, don't make it up. A storyteller spinning fiction is often easily caught in their own story and the embellishment is readily dismissed. Think upon your past and your own experiences, or those of friends and family. Keep your story not only short but true. An argument based on personal history will always have more merit than one based on philosophy and fiction.

And never forget everything we learned earlier. You established trust and found out what problem you could focus on. Whatever story you tell should call back to the problem discussed, and heighten it as something that is commonly experienced.

Opportunity 3: Giving Your Presentation

You've introduced yourself and established control. You've told your story and got them interested. Now, it's time to give them your solution. Your trial closes already have them in the mood to make a decision or commitment. Now it's time to dazzle and shine. However, presenting your opinions or product is the most crucial aspect of the process and it's something you should only do if you are in control of the situation. If you give a presentation without trust and control, then it's a waste of your breath and your prospect's time.

Now think back to that problem you identified during your introduction. The presentation is your chance to solve it. The first step should be to reiterate the problem and rephrase it in your own words, then touch on how your story related to it. Now, identify what part of your product, or philosophy, will solve that particular problem. The presentation should be focused and to the point, highlighting not only how the problem is solved, but why you are the best person to be solving it. Remember, your role as an advisor is to present the prospect with all the information they need to come to the conclusion you're guiding them to on their own. Throughout this entire process, it isn't simply the product or idea you've been selling, but your own value as well. No one will buy into what you're pitching if they don't like you.

The biggest mistake made when giving a presentation is over education. In your zeal to show how you've solved someone's problem, you usually risk giving them more information than they wanted. You solved their problem, great! Now don't go solving problems they didn't know they had. What you're pitching is usually far more complex than what anyone wants to buy. People like simplicity, and tend to think about a single issue at a time. You got them to tell you their issue, your proactive discovery helped you find the need beneath the need, and you told a story about how that issue was relatable. Now solve that issue. If you give them too much information about other facets of what you're selling, you will in most circumstances overwhelm them.

Now throughout your presentation, it's important to remember what you learned with the trial closes. Even though we're only going to focus on solving the single pressing issue, often times the solution itself will have more than one facet. So always remember that throughout the presentation you should continue to use phrases like *"That makes sense, right?"* and *"How does that sound to you?"* to continue to reinforce the commitment, and encourage affirmative agreement to the upcoming solution. The idea here is to have them completely buy in and commit before you ever ask for the sale.

Copyright © 2022 Justin O'Donnell

Opportunity 4: Closing Statements

If your trial closes were used properly, and you've established trust, then this is the easiest part of the process. You've already established a solution to the problem, and reaffirmed how your solution was the best fit. Throughout your sales process, you've used the opportunities in the introduction, story, and presentation to establish buy-in and a commitment to move forward. Now comes the most important part.

What is crucial to remember is that you never want to ask for a sale. Your position as an advisor was to get them to make the decision to buy on their own. Suggesting it as an option and a recommendation is fine, but never ask your client to buy something as if they're doing you a favor. As we discussed when outlining our sales process, we established that we want to give them an opportunity to back out, the reason for that is to confirm their commitment to following through. When you make your recommendations, rather than asking if they want to sign up, try using an affirmative statement to close. *"So now that we know how to fix our problem, let's go ahead and get you signed up today!"* We aren't asking for permission, but assuming that your prospect has bought in, and if you kept control of the conversation, and followed the process to build trust and rapport, then there's nothing you need to ask for.

They've committed, and the only thing left is the process of signing up. Whether they are buying insurance, a new car, or simply signing up for your party's email list, now is when you get them to actually put ink to paper, get that email, that phone number, or that credit card number. During this process, there shouldn't actually be much more you need to do, but affirmation and helping them complete the process, as quickly and as efficiently as possible is a must.

Opportunity 5: The Follow-Up

The most important part of closing a deal is making sure it stays closed. Most people consider following up to be something you do a few days or weeks later, but in reality, it's something you want to do before the ink even dries on the paper. If you can master the mentality that you always have to be closing, then you'll never miss the opportunity to do so. For example, let's say you're at an outreach booth signing up potential clients to be scheduled for a showing. You've got their interest and sold them on the idea of the meeting, so while they're giving you their contact information, why not go ahead and offer to schedule the meeting right then and there instead of following up later? If you're signing someone up for your political party's mailing list, then also give them information about attending your next meeting or event to learn more than you've already discussed. Silence is your wasted opportunity.

Another thing to remember when following up is the cross-sell. Anyone who has ever been sold once can be sold twice. In fact, the second time around is usually a good bit easier. You don't need to worry about building trust, just maintaining it. This is where you follow up on the second pitch. This may be a few days or weeks later, after solidifying the closing of the first pitch, but you've got them on the hook, for one thing, now offer them that next solution you held back when you first spoke. When it comes to your outreach booths especially, you already got them to sign up, and attend an event at this point, so now call on them to volunteer.

Through all of this, we've only focused on selling something to one person. But no salesperson ever paid the bills with a single sale, and no salesperson ever increased his sales by waiting for prospects to come to him. So how do we separate good salespeople from great ones? Well, that's the bread and butter of any outreach activity. One thing too few people rely on is using their existing base to grow. If you simply rely on spontaneous web traffic or walk-in customers, you'll never outgrow your current book of business. The one skill every great salesperson needs is the ability to ask for referrals. Your existing base trusted you enough to buy into what you were slinging, so now capitalize on that and get them to do the hard part of your job for you. Ask them to send their friends and family to you for help with the same problems they were having. When someone comes to you on referral, someone else laid the groundwork of trust on your behalf and made your job even easier.

What's Next?

So far we've discussed how to improve our general conversational skills, and how to take charge of those conversations once we're in them. We've touched upon the basics of a sales process and how to pitch an idea, and how to close a presentation. What's next? Well, it's time to put it into practice. Go out and find an opportunity to volunteer at an outreach event. Or take that outside business development assignment at work to get out of the office for a day. But most of all, make sure that you pay attention to yourself, don't get overwhelmed, know when to take a break, and remember what we've gone over so far. Before you were talking, but now it's time to start selling.

THE 5 TRAITS OF A SALESMAN

All the training, and practice in the world won't make you a great salesperson without adopting a few specific character traits that can change your approach to everything you do in life. We've all met someone who just has a natural talent for sales. The smooth-talking friend from college who could sell ice to an Eskimo. Yet, simply having the great conversation skills that we've previously discussed, or knowing how to control your interactions and their outcomes, isn't nearly enough to launch someone to succeed in the realm of sales. So again, whether we are selling cars, insurance, or a political ideology, it's important to be open to self-development and growth in order better ourselves and better our outcomes.

There is no end to the personality traits we could discuss, we're going to focus only on a few of them. The traits we're going to focus on are those that are easy to change and have the widest range of applications in our everyday lives as well. We will focus not only on improving our ability to sell but improving our ability to grow in the future as well, by simply focusing on five simple traits that we can start adopting today.

As we go through these traits, remember that this isn't going to be as simple to incorporate as the changes to the way we communicate as discussed earlier. These traits are things that often come naturally to some, and are much more difficult for others. It's not necessary to focus on all of them at once, but the best salespeople among us have mastered all five of them. As we go through this chapter, we are going to focus on these traits one at a time, and build upon them as we go, as opposed to implementing the changes as a whole. But by making the changes in ourselves, and being open to growth, these traits will make us better salespeople, better candidates, and better activists.

Trait 1: Positivity

Mental attitude is one of the most important aspects of any public-facing position. Whether we are working in direct sales, public outreach, or customer service, it's important to have the ability to remain positive at all times. Anyone who has ever worked in sales, or any call center environment especially, has heard the phrase "*Smile and Dial!*" This is due to a long-held belief that simply by smiling, regardless of how you actually feel, you will improve other people's perception of your attitude, voice, and tone. Simply presenting ourselves as positive, however, isn't enough to make a truly impactful change in our presentation. In order to get the full benefit from a positive attitude, we truly need to embrace positivity as a personality trait.

But why is positivity so important? Because handling failure is just as important as success. Sales is never a truly consistent environment, anyone who's ever sold can tell you that one month will be great, while the next can be down significantly. Even the greatest salespeople face rejection as often as they win, but what sets them apart is their ability to brush off the loss, learn from it, and move on.

A conversion of twenty percent is usually considered fairly high in any sales position, so that means that even the best salespeople get rejected over eighty percent of the time. So when you follow your process and do everything right, occasionally you will still fail to convert a prospect, it's important that you can take that loss, embrace it, learn from it, move on and be positive. Bring positive energy to everything you do, and even in failure, you'll be successful.

Trait 2: Eagerness To Learn

We should all strive to embrace a lifelong student mentality anyways, regardless of the position, field, or career we are pursuing. However, it's crucial in sales and activism. The willingness to learn and improve yourself is one of the best qualities we can have in our lives, and the fact that you are reading this book is indicative of a great start, but it's just the beginning. When I was first getting started in sales, the agent that was training me used to ask every single Monday, what book I was reading that week. He didn't actually care what book I was reading, but always wanted to ensure that I was reading something in my free time to learn, grow and improve myself, and I'm a better person today because of it.

In order to progress and succeed, you need to be willing to learn and grow as a person and a professional. Whether you are an executive or a new trainee, you should always be looking for people around you who do things differently and figure out what works for them. If that new guy is outperforming you on his first day, sure it could be beginner's luck, or it could be that he's approaching things with a new perspective that you hadn't thought of yet.

So be the student you need to be, embrace alternative methods, and be willing to learn, even from the most inexperienced around you. We often talk about how successful people surround themselves with other successful people, but I approach things from the school of thought that it doesn't matter who you surround yourself with, successful people are those who can learn something from anyone they interact with.

Trait 3: Grind and Hustle

The high-performing professionals are the hardest working people you know. We all know someone that stands out with this trait. They are usually the first to show up and last to leave, and they don't think twice about working through breaks to get something done. These are the people that understand that taking the extra time to prepare before getting to work will set you up for a more productive day, and taking the extra time when you're done will give you the opportunity to put things in order and tie up loose ends before going home. In any sales environment, you're always going to get out what you put in, and when you put in the extra effort, you get out the extra rewards.

This is especially true for activists and those working in outreach. Showing up to events early to get set up, and staying beyond the time you originally signed up for, just to make sure there's coverage. The activist with the strongest work ethic is the one who's going to be following up on leads gathered from events, and being the face of the movement.

It's not a surprise that the hardest working people amongst us become the most influential. The leaders, the managers, the ones who rise to the top, are the ones most willing to put everything they have into their work. A strong work ethic is important not only for the success of your work but for your success in daily life. So get out and grind, put your shoes on the pavement, wake up early and put yourself out there. If you put in the work, don't be surprised to see things trend upwards.

Copyright © 2022 Justin O'Donnell

Step 4: Be Professional

As a salesman, you are the public-facing image representing your brand or company. As an activist, the same is true for being the representative of your entire philosophy. Whether you are a first-timer or a veteran, those you interact with will see you as the ambassador for all things you represent. So rather than deflecting this responsibility, it's imperative that you embrace it instead. Understand the importance of your own professionalism in the situation, and work towards being the best you that you can be.

Evaluating your own professionalism, and improving upon it, is an incredibly objective action. You should look at the total picture available, and identify the things you would judge others for in order to make the changes necessary. The little things can make the biggest impact in this endeavor. Watch your language, and speak calmly and professionally at all times. Mind your personal hygiene, and be sure to not offend the sensibilities of those you interact with. And just as importantly, dress smartly and appropriately for each situation. How you present yourself is just as important as what you have to say. All good salespeople know that when they are working, everything they do must be in the best interests of the brand or company they are representing.

Step 5: Be Hungry

In order to achieve something, you must want to achieve it. In order to excel at something, you must have the will to dedicate what is necessary to do so. If you want to make it to the top in any field, then you need to be willing to put in the effort. Sales and politics are no different in these regards. Either field will require immense personal dedication and commitment to what you do if you want to succeed.

This trait is a fundamental necessity of the others we've discussed. And it's crucial that it's understood that in any aspect of life if you are to succeed at anything, you must first want to. In order to be driven, you must be hungry, and you must be willing to feed your hunger for success.

The Change

These five traits are something we find in our top leaders, politicians, salespeople, and athletes. When we are driving towards success, we must be positive, willing to learn, willing to put in the hours, cognizant of our presentation, and hungry for success. But unlike adapting our conversational skills, adopting these traits will be much more difficult, and require much more dedication, but it's worth it to aim for success.

THE 7 SKILLS OF SUCCESS

Apart from adopting certain personality traits and embracing good conversational tactics, there are certain skills that the best salespeople have mastered in every facet of their professions and lives. These skills are things that anyone can work to incorporate into their daily lives and their professional relationships, and build off the conversational skills we discussed when we first began.

These skills will complement your newfound conversational skills, and allow you to extend your control of social and political situations even further.

The ability to be comfortable in any manner of conversation, debate, argument, or interaction, will be crucial in your journey to becoming the best salesperson you can be. But as shown by the theme of our previous lessons, the key to any sales success is a foundation in communications.

    You can't make any sale until you've demonstrated value to your prospect. Only then will they trust you enough to tell you their problems, and buy into your solutions for them. So let's take a deeper look at the communication skills of success, that will bring our sales games to the next level.

Skill 1: Be Curious

We've covered listening skills several times so far, and there's a lot more to say about them than we've had the chance to go over. That's because the ability to listen is arguably one of the most important skills a salesperson can have, and equally for any conversation or relationship, whether business or personal. But what we're discussing here isn't merely the importance of listening or even the intent of it. What matters with this skill is the ability to genuinely care about what your prospect has to say. You can never be too curious when it comes to interactions with clients and prospects.

If you have properly built trust with the person you're speaking to, then there shouldn't be anything of note that they would hesitate to share with you. So within the context of the conversation you are having, ask the questions you want answers to, and pay attention to the details of their answers. It's important that you balance your curiosity with active listening skills and not let the conversation get away from the matter at hand.

Remember to give your full and utter attention to the matter at hand, and not let yourself get distracted, even if it's your prospect that runs the risk of distracting you. Use your curiosity to guide the conversation, but keep sure to not let it be detracted. Too often an impatient sales rep is just waiting for their turn to talk and using the opportunity to plan their next comment as opposed to actually listening to what their prospect has to say. And by devoting your honest curiosity and attention to the conversation, you have the opportunity to ask relevant follow-up questions that keep the conversation on track and satisfy your need for more information as well. Oftentimes, it won't be what the prospect actually says that reveals what you're looking for, but by paying attention you are able to notice the nuances of their body language as well.

Skill 2: Empathize

Nothing sets you up to better speak to a prospect, than understanding their circumstance and seeing things from their point of view. Even if you disagree with the point they're making, the ability to understand the rationale behind it allows you to speak more clearly about the issue as they view it. The ability to empathize with your prospects will help you in building trust, and enhance your end of the conversations you are having as well.

Displaying empathy is far more complicated than simply telling them that you understand what they are going through. The best salespeople are those who actually understand the situations and problems of their prospects, and are actually familiar with their experiences. When you have an understanding of the problems faced on a daily basis in an industry, then you are uniquely suited to represent your brand to that sector, and shouldn't let that opportunity go to waste.

There is one particular tool that you have at your disposal at all times, and it is something far harder to master than you realize, even though you've used it every day of your life. Your voice and the manner in which you speak are something that salespeople are particularly adept at manipulating.

One of the biggest aspects of empathy is comfort and making the prospect feel familiar. The idea is to meet them on their grounds, even when it's in your office. When presented with a prospect who speaks slowly, then soften your own tone and match the speed of their words. If you are engaged with someone who speaks a mile a minute, then turn up the excitement and match their enthusiasm. By speaking in a manner that your prospect is comfortable with, you increase the odds that the words you say will be understood as intended.

So build on your experiences, and embrace the connections you can build with your prospects. By emphasizing your empathic abilities, and using skills such as body language and voice tone to make prospects more comfortable, you will be better suited to get your message across and close the deal.

Skill 3: Don't Make Assumptions

Routine is the death of any sale. You might think that when you met a thousand people, then you've met them all, but the assumption that everyone you talk to will be the same is a fatal mistake. We all like patterns, and we all like to simplify the processes we go through. Just because the first 100 people you speak to at an event are all from the same background, don't be surprised when the 101st is offended when you use that as an icebreaker.

Unless the prospect has personally told you something, or you have other verifiable sources of information, then never assume that the information you are working with is complete and valid. Each and every interaction you have is unique and new and independent of any and all past conversations that you have had. If you are uncertain of a piece of background information, then simply ask for clarification. Use your conversational skills to find the information in a friendly manner, but never assume something about someone you don't know. Asking a follow-up question may break your script, and interrupt your streamlined pitch, but it shows a human element of the salesperson and shows the prospect that you care about their individuality as opposed to making assumptions regarding their situation. However, making a prospect feel ignored, or having them interrupt you to correct what you've said, can damage the integrity of your position and destroy any trust you've built up to that point.

Skill 4: Read Between the Lines

Sometimes you are going to get the prospects to trust you implicitly, and won't have to worry about them leaving out information that's important to the process. This is common in business-to-consumer sales and personal outreach in politics. Situations where trust is easy to establish, and the dominance of a conversation is very one-sided in favor of the salesperson. However, sometimes you'll face prospects that are more guarded, less trusting, and who will withhold information in an attempt to retain a bit of control in the situation. This is more common in business-to-business sales, and debates and arguments in the political realm. However, don't assume it won't happen in direct sales or personal conversations, and when it does, don't assume it's always intentional or done in bad faith. Sometimes, people leave out details they don't think are important, because their understanding differs from yours, not out of malice.

Prospects withholding information is fine and doesn't impact your ability to work with them, so long as you are able to recognize the fact that it's happening. There could be a number of reasons as to why someone withholds information, but the most common will be because they don't fully trust you. Or sometimes it isn't an issue of trust, but rather circumstance. Perhaps you've been speaking to a gentleman about a product you are selling, and he's convinced and bought in on all your trial closes, but still won't pull the trigger and close the deal. Most likely, it's because you've been speaking to the wrong person. He wasn't the ultimate decision maker in the conversation, you sold him, but you didn't pick up on the fact that his wife who wasn't present, was the one who would ultimately make the final decision..

Learning to read between the lines will augment your curiosity and make it much easier to get a firm grasp of the situation at hand before you spend too much time going down the wrong road. It will allow you to find the hidden details that someone might not have willingly given up for one reason or another, and use them to better your own position in the conversation. This skill can help you in any conversation, professionally or personally, so long as you don't get cocky and abuse it. If you start looking for hidden meanings, you run the risk of making the wrong assumptions.

Skill 5: Assume Good Intent

Sometimes a deal falls through for inexplicable reasons. Sometimes the details that were withheld change the nature of the solution. Sometimes, you convinced one person, but not the eventual decision maker. Sometimes, your prospect just lied and misled you on purpose. While all of these situations are extraordinarily frustrating, they are not all malicious and intentional.

It's often difficult to ascertain whether or not the prospect is acting with malice in mind if you weren't able to read thoroughly between the lines earlier. While we may often want to assume that those who caused us an annoyance were the reason we failed to close the deal, the truth is, the majority of the time it was straying from our process or losing control of the conversation that caused us to fail, and not any action by the prospect. If you fall into the trap of blaming your prospects for the mistakes you make in the sales process, you run the risk of creating a subconscious assumption and treating all of your prospects as if they are hostile. This kind of mental trap can lead you into treating conversations as debates and will derail your sales process and leave you unable to close.

We counter the malicious prospects not by treating them any differently, but by being the more trusting partner. We assume good intent in all those we speak with and give them the opportunity to prove us right, as opposed to waiting for them to prove us wrong. But just because we assume good intent in our prospects doesn't mean they assume the same of us. There is a natural, cultural aversion to salespeople and their tactics. The easiest way to put your prospects at ease, and get them to trust you, is, to be honest from the very beginning. Your prospects won't be upfront with you unless they trust you, so this means you have to be entirely upfront with them about what you don't know so that when you do know something, they trust it implicitly.

Skill 6: Be The Expert

Nobody becomes a top car salesman by speaking in broad generalizations, and dramatic rhetoric. A great used car salesperson gets you on the hook by talking about the specifics of the product at hand. They can point to specific features of the car they are trying to sell and highlight the point they are trying to make, about how that feature will solve their customer's problem. In sales and politics alike, you want to be as specific as possible without weighing down the conversation in detail. Highlight what's important, relate it with an anecdote, solve the problem and move on. Be as specific as you can with the solution, and don't rely on fun catchphrases alone to get you a sale.

However, you can't be specific if you don't know what you are talking about. If you are selling to a specific industry or doing outreach to an issues-based group, you have to make sure that you are a subject, and issue matter expert, because if you aren't, then your prospects will be. A prospect will never trust you if you don't understand their business or their issues, so rely on your ability to empathize, and use references to past prospects that you have converted to establish credibility, but be wary of the risk you run of losing it if you can't answer the simple questions.

Skill 7: Know What You Don't Know

The most important part of being an expert is knowing what you don't know. The so-called experts who never miss a beat when answering questions are great for trivia, but their confidence can be shaken thoroughly when presented with a single question they don't know the answer to. We've gone over this before, and there really isn't much more to it. But remember the simplicity and the importance of this message.

Know what you don't know, and say what you don't know because not knowing is better than being wrong. There is nothing wrong with telling a prospect that you don't have the answer, but that you will get it for them. But getting caught in a lie will destroy any trust you have previously built. One underused tactic, that requires a good bit of control in the conversation, is relying on your customers and prospects to fill the gaps in your own knowledge. The prospect will appreciate your honesty and feel more included in the process when there is a back and forth.

Follow Through

All the skills we have discussed so far, from starting a conversation, to closing a difficult sale, culminate with you working towards implementing these skills in your everyday personal and professional lives. While some things may be easy to change, like putting your phone away at the dinner table, some might be more difficult, like committing more time and effort to your tasks. Regardless, we are now on the road to becoming better activists and salespeople, and the only thing left is crafting our message.

12 Keys to Winning and Losing Debates

At this point, we've established some rules and skills for getting the most out of our conversations and sales process to convert those we speak with and sell them our message. While these skills will allow you to have more productive and enjoyable conversations with those you encounter in life, not everyone will engage you in willing conversation. There's always the chance you run into someone whose mind simply will not be changed.

This circumstance isn't the time to try and have a conversation, but it is an opportunity to have a debate. And an opportunity isn't always something you should take just because it's offered. The biggest part of winning a debate is knowing when it's worth having. Most debates won't be formal events with time to prepare and agreed-upon rules and structure. In fact, most debates are nothing more than informal arguments in the public sphere. If the scenario is private, with no audience, then it is much better set for a conversation if one can be had, but if you are engaged by someone intent on arguing publicly, then knowing how to win the debate is just as important as the ability to have a conversation

Before you can win a debate, you must first know who the audience is, because that is who you are actually speaking to. In most circumstances, someone who engages you philosophically will not be of the mind to change their opinions based solely on your argument. Winning the debate doesn't mean you changed your opponent's mind, but rather that you have influenced those watching whose minds aren't already made up. So dust off your facts and get ready for twelve steps to win your next debate

Step 1: Stay Calm

Arguments and debates are known to get emotionally charged and full of steam. Allowing yourself to succumb to this is a sure way to give up your composure and lose the argument. Even when your opponent uses baseless personal attacks or illogical arguments, it's important that you remain level-headed at all times. And while passion and excitement are great allies in both conversation and debate alike, it doesn't matter how passionate you are about your points, maintaining command of your emotions will keep you in control of the debate.

Those who debate on emotional grounds often gain early dominance in an argument, but rarely win. We've all been in fights where we subconsciously knew that all we had to do to win was stay calm. The person we were arguing with would get so riled up that they would eventually quit. The moment someone starts yelling, you know you've won, but that doesn't mean the debate is over.

Simply remaining calm isn't enough, and the other person losing their temper alone doesn't mean you're out of the fight just yet either. Typically when someone loses their temper, they will double down on previous arguments, and resort to underhanded debate tactics. It's important to maintain composure and beware of what tactics might be used against you as well.

Step 2: Back It Up

When you engage in debate or argument, it's a defense of the positions as opposed to a discussion of them. Each and every claim you make will be questioned and attacked, so you must be prepared to back them up. Know your sources, and don't wait for them to ask you for citations. When you make a factual claim in support of your argument, preface it with the source of the fact. Facts are very difficult to refute, so it helps to be prepared for these circumstances by knowing the defense of your points from all angles.

It also matters what sources you are citing, as not all polling firms or news sources are created equally. Being able to cite something from The Pew Research Center will have significantly more impact than Survey monkey or your local newspaper. Quotes from historical figures are valid, but contentious without context, as they generally display a known bias as well. If your point can be supported by unbiased, and nonpartisan news sources and academic studies, then you are best served to rely solely on them, as opposed to the political acumen of your aunt on Facebook.

Step 3: Ask Questions

For the same reason you need to be able to defend your own positions, you must be willing and ready to challenge your opponents. The ability to ask open-ended leading questions will better you in catching your opponent off guard and being unable to defend their positions.

This goes back to maintaining control. By asking questions you're able to force the debate to focus on the topics you want to cover. If you can control both the narrative and the pace of the debate, you are in a stronger position to influence a more desirable outcome. So make sure you're prepared not just to answer questions when challenged, but ask them of your opponent as well.

There are a number of different types of leading questions you can ask to influence how your opponent debates. Ask questions that challenge their point, '*What evidence do you have for that claim?*' Ask a hypothetical question that extrapolates a trend and gives your opponent a difficult situation, '*What would happen if every nation did that?*' Or ask a question designed to capitalize on emotions and provoke them into losing control, '*What is about this that makes you so angry?*'

Step 4: Connect The Dots

The beauty of logical philosophies is that when emotions are controlled, they are easily followed and make their own case. So deconstruct your own arguments, and break them down to the fundamental logic that supports them. Be familiar with the simplest arguments possible that support your philosophy. When you are defending your philosophy and making your arguments, do so in a manner that follows the logical progression as your complete philosophy is reconstructed.

By allowing logic to guide your argument, you make it easy to follow and difficult to attack. Because if your opponent wants to attack something logical, they would have to attack the basis of logic itself. While logic does fail to convince some people on its own, those who aren't willing to cast it aside for morality and emotions need nothing except simple logical progression to cede the point.

    However, be careful to avoid simply presenting the varying points, and pieces of the puzzle, without connecting them. Never assume your audience has both the willingness and capacity to reasonably ascertain the underlying points of your argument. As each new piece of information is presented to your argument, you must also take what time you can to explain how they connect and walk the listener through the progression to your final position. A failure to reasonably articulate the connections could leave a listener with disjointed information, and a misunderstanding waiting to happen.

Step 5: Take The High Ground

The only case where logic fails is when the audience is captivated by emotions. People are inherently irrational, and emotional beings, and often can't follow the logical process when an argument tugs at the heartstrings. Because of this, it behooves you to claim the moral high ground as early as possible in a debate.

When we appeal to the higher values of humanity with our argument, we can lay early claim to the moral imperative. By framing our arguments in a manner that emphasizes motives based on shared values, we create a circumstance where disagreeing with us is not only irrational but cruel at its core. After all, shouldn't we all be working to make the world better and safer for our children? It's easier to take that stance than to refute it, especially when emotions rule the argument.

Should we unwittingly cede the high ground and let our opponent combat our proposals as harmful to the shared ethics and morals of the audience, then the difficulty in overcoming emotions to win with our logic can become insurmountable. Think of the most common arguments each day in our current political scheme. Proponents of healthcare reform don't say they support it because they care about people, but they say others oppose it because they don't care about people. Gun rights activists don't care about children, and pro-life activists don't care about women. This form of negative moral high ground is an offensive measure, meant to delegitimize your points before they ever get the chance to be made.

Step 6: Keep Listening

We've already spent a good deal of time going over the importance of listening, but that doesn't diminish this point. Lyndon B. Johnson said that *"You aren't learning anything when you're talking."* and this is especially important to remember when debating. In order to refute points made by your opponent, you need to actually hear them, understand them, and learn the strengths and weaknesses of their arguments.

While listening is equally important in conversations and debates, the reasoning is different. Whereas before, we were listening with the goal of understanding and empathy in order to be better conversationalists and better salespeople, now we are listening to dissect, target, and respond. Be conscious of every point made by your opponent, so you can be better prepared to answer them. Listening intently will allow you to properly respond and question your opponent.

One of the easiest things to listen out for is any point or connection your opponent tries to make, that may inadvertently lend credibility to your own stances. If you can make a case that your opponent is actually in agreement with your underlying point, you can place the onus on them to refute their own logic and emotional reasoning. A well-timed and placed challenge could cause the audience to doubt the authenticity and integrity of the claims they're being presented, and to consider yours when they had otherwise made up their minds.

Step 7: Give Them Credit

No argument is perfect, not even yours. And no argument is entirely wrong, not even theirs. If you debate enough, then eventually you will find an opponent who is more prepared than you. Yet, regardless of preparation, it is inevitable that every once in a while, your opponent will make a good point. Make sure you are prepared for that to happen.

When your opponent makes such a point, then don't brush it off, and definitely don't ignore it. Sometimes, they'll even make a point that you agree with, and this is something that you have an opportunity to capitalize on. What you'll want to do, rather than dismissing their good point, or claiming it as a '*got ya!*' moment, I acknowledge the agreement and highlight the divergence.

When a point is made, break it down, acknowledge it, and refute it not with dismissal, but by furthering the initial claim. Build upon the point your opponent made in a manner that supports your own argument instead. Do so by starting with an open agreement, explaining where you disagree at the next junction of logic, and finishing with a statement that returns the point to your message instead of theirs. Being prepared for this possibility will allow you to avoid being caught undermining the integrity of your argument by acknowledging the distinction in understanding the same logical argument.

Step 8: Do Your Homework

Not always a possibility in spur-of-the-moment arguments, with prepared debates you have the opportunity to not only prepare your argument but to prepare for your opponent as well. Knowing how your opponent debates, the arguments they prefer to make, and the style they usually argue, can prepare you to counter them. When you are familiar with your opponent's weaknesses you can easily exploit them to turn their own arguments against them.

In a circumstance where you can't prepare for the opponent directly, it is imperative that you prepare for the arguments you will face. Knowing your own philosophy isn't enough to win a debate, but a thorough understanding of the philosophy that opposes you is needed as well. When you understand the arguments that will be used against you, including their justifications, their rationale, their connections, and logic then it is much easier to craft a response tailored to catch your opponent off guard.

In the same vein of thought, it's important that you understand each and every flaw of your own arguments as well. The knowledge that your own argument is imperfect will allow you to be prepared when your opponent attacks, knowing what they will say, and being able to craft a rationalization to negate their point. We call this opposition research, and campaign teams will usually have a debate expert dedicated solely to this task, in order to prepare candidates for the hard questions.

By doing our homework, and being fully prepared to know our opponents, and their arguments, we set ourselves up to succeed and not only be prepared but feel prepared for the debate as well. When entering any argument, the confidence of preparedness will help us maintain control of ourselves, our emotions, and our debate.

Step 9: Move the Needle

Knowing how rare and difficult it will be to actually change the mind of someone arguing against us, you must be prepared to cede ground and give up to credible arguments for a reason. You must remember to be open-minded to the possibility of a compromise solution that accommodates points made by you and your opponent both. When we acknowledge reasonable compromises, we move the needle in the right direction, by getting your opponent to cede to some of your points as well. Remember, when we engage in debate, we do it to speak to the audience bearing witness.

If both parties in the debate stick to their guns implicitly, then it will create an air of hostility surrounding the debate. Those paying attention will hear great points from both sides, but in reality, they care more about the people debating than the debate itself. By showing the willingness to meet on common ground, you reinforce your claim to the moral high ground and endear yourself to the audience. Remember that the goal of engaging in the debate was never to convince the other party that they were wrong, but to convince those watching to consider your position. Even if they only consider a portion of your position at the end of the day, then you've made progress towards winning them over.

Step 10: Stick to the Issues

The biggest trap in the debate is also becoming the most common flaw in all arguments, big and small. When we abandon our issue-based arguments we're left with only one option left - personal attacks.

Direct attacks against your opponent, their lifestyle, honesty, integrity, or past should be avoided entirely. When you make a personal attack, you give up any claim to moral superiority. When you make personal attacks you admit that your arguments aren't put together well enough to stand up to the criticism of your opponent, so you rely on attacking their credibility instead. If you truly believe in the philosophy you purport, then do not devalue it by losing your decorum in this debate. The worst consequence of engaging in personal attacks is the possibility that those in the audience who identify with your opponent's view, may take the attacks as commentary on themselves as well as your opponent. If this happens, you've lost all chance of winning them over to your side.

Step 11: Don't Get Distracted

When your opponent feels they've lost on a particular point, and there's nothing they can gain by continuing to argue it, they will often try to change the subject or introduce a new point to distract from their argument. It is easy to allow yourself to be distracted and fall into their trap, but you have to remember to stick to the issue at hand. Given the evolving nature of debates and arguments, you can't be sure you'll have the opportunity to return to a previous point that was left unfinished.

You must remain firm to stop such detraction. Stuck to your guns and circle back to make your point before allowing the conversation to move on. The simple response is *"That is an entirely different issue, let's focus on the matter at hand for now."*

Step 12: Know Your Strengths

Everyone has their strengths and weaknesses, even you. It is crucially important that you know what yours are when going into an argument or debate. And while your personal strengths are important, your argumentative weaknesses are even more so. Going back to doing your homework and knowing the arguments inside and out from both sides, it's imperative you know which of your arguments and points are the strongest.

If you know that you have a handful of strong, irrefutable points, simply focus on them, and use your conversational skills to control the direction of the debate to focus on them. Once you've made your points and argued them convincingly, ask for agreement and end the debate. If you allow the debate to continue past your strengths, you run the risk of losing what you've already won.

Should you be drawn into arguing points you aren't as prepared for, then you run the risk of presenting weaker arguments that aren't as convincing. When this happens, then you give your opponent the ability to easily rebut your weak arguments and take back control of the debate. In this event, you've not only lost on those points where you weren't prepared, but you run the risk of watering down the entirety of your argument and making the case for your side look weaker by comparison.

Know Your Setting

While these steps will help better prepare you for debate, it's still crucial that you know when they need to apply. An argument between two individuals is very different from a debate in front of an audience. These tips are best used for the setting of a debate, and regardless of hostility, a one-on-one conversation should be focused on the skills we worked on for conversations. But regardless of the setting, there is one final piece of advice that will serve you well, always maintain a sense of humor in your arguments.

Tuning Your Marketing

One of the most undervalued parts of the sales process is initial marketing and advertising. A salesperson can only sell their product if they have prospects to sell it to. With a good marketing campaign, the prospects will seek you out, and you'll never have downtime to worry about what you're going to do next. However, inversely, a bad marketing campaign will leave a sour taste, and preconceptions of your product in the minds of the prospects you're left to seek out. Whether your marketing includes tv commercials, direct mail campaigns, or just public statements made by representatives of your organization, it sets the initial understanding and expectations of what you are selling. Your success as a salesperson, or as an activist, will be either helped or hindered by the message conveyed in your marketing materials and outreach.

    This is where sales and politics will diverge in the necessity, but not necessarily in tactics. In sales, your marketing is designed to generate interest in a product, whereas in politics your marketing should be designed to generate doubt in your prospect's existing philosophy. And while sales marketing is usually focused on traditional media, politics is inherently more focused on individual personalities. The candidates and organizational leaders involved in politics inherently have gravity to their position. So whether you are running for Congress, or are the Vice Chair of a political party, the individual actions and statements you make will have more of an impact on the organization's marketing than if you were an executive with a company.

    When it comes to marketing for a political organization, the task is never done, and it is never impersonal. As a representative of a political organization, you must be aware of the fact that everything you say will be broken down and ridiculed, and must take care that your public statements, whether spoken or written, can only be construed in the best interest of the movement and the organization. There are some among us who take the view that simply getting attention is better than being ignored, even if the reason we're getting attention is that our messaging was misconstrued as offensive and improper.

When we make public statements, we may be inclined to speak in radical overtones, to make as much noise and garner as much attention as possible. While we will certainly succeed in being villainized, unless our goals do not include recruiting, growth, and eventually winning elections, then what we accomplish is usually detrimental to our own cause. It is important to remember that we will never grow or expand our audience if we only speak to those already on board with our messaging.

Now I'm not saying we shouldn't keep our marketing principled and on message, but we need to take care to make sure that what we say presents the radical messaging we want to share in a manner that encourages those who don't already agree with us to think about what we have to say and investigate further. When we tone our messaging in a manner that speaks only to reinforce the views of those who already agree with us, we drive away new prospects, who could have potentially been converted to lending their support.

The goal of any marketing effort should be to increase outreach, develop interest, and put your salespeople into contact with the prospects you are targeting for conversion. So whether in corporate sales or politics, our eventual goal with marketing will remain the same, even if the avenues of outreach are different. the 5 steps involved in tuning a message for proper marketing still remain the same: Identifying your audience, Identifying their problems, Offering help, Referencing success, and establishing yourself as unique.

Step 1: Identify Your Target Audience

The first step in crafting your message is to identify who it is you want to hear your message and figure out who actually will hear it. In corporate sales, you can usually rest assured that your advertising and marketing will not exceed its intended scope, but in politics, there is no such guarantee, so you should generally be very broad with your assumption of who the audience will be. The ideal target audience though should always be those who aren't already aware of your product or message. Your existing customers don't need to be marketed to as much as those who have never heard of you. If you tailor your message only to those who have already bought in, then you run the risk of alienating those who haven't.

Every successful business has a target market, the difficulty for a political organization is identifying the target audience that isn't your existing base. While this can certainly be broad on specific issue-based outreach, like veterans, gun owners, or the LGBTQ community, I would advise that as those in organizational leadership positions, we should craft our messaging to speak towards our total target audience, as opposed to just a single aspect of it. And most of all, we should take care to remain principled and engage our political base of supporters, while not relying on hostile messaging that drives away those who could possibly join their ranks. Using such a broad scope to define our audience will hinder our ability to craft succinct messaging, but it is the politically smart thing to do in order to grow the base that supports our core messaging.

Step 2: Identify Their Problems

Once you've identified the target market, then you need to figure out what problems it is they face. What problems do they have, and how do those problems make them feel? Sound familiar? It should, your marketing strategy will closely resemble the sales process itself. But the frustrations experienced by your chosen target market will impact how they view marketing strategies that are presented to them. And if you can identify a problem, and focus on that problem with your messaging, then you are more apt to have someone who experiences that problem pay attention to what you have to say. People don't care about what you have to say until they know you care about how they feel. By focusing your marketing efforts on highlighting problems that people experience every day, then it tells those same people that not only do you understand the problem, but you empathize with them and care about how they handle those problems.

The secret to crafting a good marketing campaign for a sales professional includes ensuring that your message is something that gets someone's interest, and encourages them to inquire further. For a political activist, your messaging will have the same fundamental goal, even though your primary method of outreach will be your own words and public statements as opposed to commercial advertising. The easiest way to grab the attention and interest of someone is to highlight a problem that they understand and experience.

Step 3: Offer Help

Getting someone's attention, and making them aware of an issue at hand isn't enough in its own right to be considered successful marketing. At this point, all you've done is highlighted a problem, but that isn't anything that your prospects weren't already aware of. Now it's time to offer a solution. Because what people really want is for their problems to be solved.

When you present a solution to someone's problem, you not only get their explicit interest but in some cases will encourage a suspension of disbelief in the prospect as well. People are so wanting for their problems to be solved, that when you present your solution as a simple cure for all that ails them, there's a chance that they'll buy in fully based solely on the promise. So be sure to simply, and succinctly explain all the benefits of your solution and how it will eliminate the problems and anguish you've already identified for your prospect.

If you remember all the way back to our IMPACT Sales Process, we discussed the importance of finding the need beneath the need. During a sale, you'll explain to your prospect how your solution fixes their problem by addressing the hidden problems they might not have been aware of, but that you've educated them about. However, when we're simply marketing ourselves, getting too into the weeds of the matter can actually become a distraction. So keep our offer to help succinct and simple. We're solving problems, ask us how.

Step 4: Reference Success

While it's totally possible that prospects viewing your promotional material will buy in solely because they are intrigued by the solutions you offer, more than likely that alone isn't enough to establish any credibility to your claims. When we make a claim that seems too good to be true, many people are still going to assume that it is. That pending doubt can be assuaged by calling on past successes, and referencing the viability and effectiveness of your solutions as presented.

In corporate sales, you might be familiarized with customer testimonials and other tactics that fulfill this need. This is not only common but effective. When you identify a problem and offer a solution, people do naturally want to be reassured that your solution works. While an insurance company or car salesperson might choose to focus on customer testimonials and market share impact, those may not be readily available to all political entities. What you often will have available to you is legal precedent and social experiments in other jurisdictions. When I hear social activists arguing for the ending of the drug war as a solution to social, budgetary, and other issues we face as a country, one of the strongest arguments they have at their disposal is to call upon the evidence of programs in countries like Portugal, where the implementation of the program they are suggesting was extraordinarily successful.

So do your research, and don't forget to take notes and make note of the details you'll need to defend your positions. Be able to defend your solutions with evidence of their success, and know the results that have been achieved. People will be much more willing to support a solution or buy into a product once it can be shown to them that it has worked for others already, and they aren't going to be taking a risk without evidentiary support.

Step 5: How Are You Different?

The ultimate goal of a marketing campaign is to get your prospects in touch with your salespeople, and at this point, we've gotten their attention, identified a problem, and promised to solve it. But so has every other competitor. What is it that sets you apart from your competition, from the other dealership down the street, or from your political opponents? This is one of the more crucial aspects of marketing, making sure that you aren't advertising for your opponents and competition.

You need to communicate your differences, but make sure to stay positive with them. Don't go out of your way to name the competition in your marketing, or else you'll drive your prospect to seek them out as well for competing information. So avoid attacking and highlighting the problems that they face, and instead focus on what is so great and special about you. Have you won any awards? Do you have a record of success? Or are you a newcomer with bright ideas, and a clean slate? Whatever it is that sets you apart, frame it in a positive manner and make sure you let your prospects know about it. After all, it's your solution, you should be the one to implement it.

The Messaging Mistake

Now that we have a framework of how to craft a marketing message, and an understanding of who are audience is and how they'll view us, it's time to talk about what message we convey with that medium. There are several ways your message can come across when following this formula, and the differences will be subtle but impactful. When your prospect views your marketing, they are going to think that you are either explaining what you do or telling them what's in it for them. There is an obvious preference in what we want to convey.

When someone here's our message but the marketing is driven on focusing on what we do, then we failed to properly capture their attention with the problems and focused too heavily on our presentation of our solution. However, when we get the balance of those two right, we not only showcase the options we provide, but we also make the prospect ask the most basic of questions, "*What's in it for me?*"

That's the fundamental question we want to answer when we provide our solution and sell ourselves as the proper provider of that solution. When we can get prospects to see our presentation as an invitation of self-interest, then they'll be the ones who pick up the phone and search you out. Because remember, the goal of marketing is to give the salespeople someone to work with.

Now Put It All Together

So there we have it, a simplified understanding of a basic sales process and marketing strategy, and how it can be applied to political activism in the real world. This strategy, while simplified, and very basic, will fundamentally transform the way we speak to others, and each other, and encourage us to have better conversations, and win the debates that matter. But these skills will only help if we put them into place. So whether you work in software engineering or customer service, or even if you have a background in sales yourself, try these steps we've discussed and see if they can create any positive changes in your life. We all deserve to be having better conversations with those around us.

Once we can make the change in our everyday lives and improve our ability to have conversations with those we interact with on a daily basis, then we can shift towards a practice of controlling those conversations with those we deal with in a professional or political setting. This is where we stop becoming activists and start becoming salespeople. But our connection to the political mission doesn't die with these changes. In fact, if anything we reinforce it.

Because we aren't learning or employing these skills for financial gain, or notoriety, but to make a positive change in the world we live in. We are in this to make an impact, win the debate, and lead the conversation about our future. But if you forget everything we talked about, and take nothing else away from this book, then do yourself a favor, shut up and listen!

Moving the Overton Window

Created by academic and policy analyst Joseph P. Overton in the mid-1990s, the Overton Window is a representative model of how the acceptance of ideas in society changes over time, and how those ideas impact politics and policy. Society dictates what is considered acceptable, and politicians act within that sphere. The Overton window charts ideas from one extreme to another, encapsulating somewhere what society deems reasonable somewhere in between. Overton, a libertarian himself, initially proposed his theory by plotting ideas on an axis ranging from Total freedom with No Government regulation to Total tyranny with complete government control.

The general premise of the window is that to judge the political viability of an idea, you need to determine its popularity. Overton remarked that the success of a political idea was independent of a politician's personal preferences, but rather the acceptability of the idea to the people responsible for electing the politician. While this does reinforce the running theory that politicians as a class are largely devoid of principles, it lends credence to the beliefs that policy can in fact be influenced by public will.

When an idea exists inside the Overton window, it is generally accepted to be pursued as policy by legislators and politicians. When an idea exists outside the Overton window, then it is publicly unthinkable to propose or support it. Knowing this, we can tailor our approach to public policy, by focusing on bringing our ideas into consideration of mass appeal using the Overton Window. But to do so, we need to understand it, how it works, how it moves, and know where we are in relation to where we want to be.

The Axis of Freedom

The Overton window is generally presented by plotting ideas along an axis. To keep things both simple and relatable, we'll use the axis as defined by Joseph Overton himself. Overton presented his theory as an axis on which any policy proposal could be situated from "More Free" to "Less Free." A scale of relative freedom should be easy to understand for most libertarians, but for others, this scale has been referenced as a degree of government regulation involved in a particular policy. On the "More Free" end of the spectrum, policies would typically advocate for minimal, if any, government regulation regarding the issue, and on the "Less Free" end of the scale would lie policies that inherently require more directly involved regulation from the state.

With the extremes of each end being generally

opposed, they are quite simply, unthinkable. However, a slightly less extreme idea might be simply radical, and then less extreme than radical would be acceptable, followed by sensible, then popular, and right in the middle, is the status quo. But the status quo isn't the end, as the spectrum of acceptability shifts downward in the other direction you just came from among the same progression. The job of politicians, at least as they see it, is to identify and advocate for those policies most acceptable to the greater population as determined by the Overton window.

At its purest, the Overton window is simply a tool by which to describe the acceptability of an idea and to measure the movement of public sentiment. And that's the real key because public sentiment can shift, and so can the status quo and the entire Overton Window.

Moving the Needle

The Overton window can shift, it can expand, and it can contract. It is not a stable standard by which eternal judgment of ideas can be made. The number of ideas within the Overton window, and their inclination towards more or less freedom will be fluid based on constantly shifting public perception of them. Politicians often won't risk supporting a policy that lies outside the Overton Window, but sometimes will try and encourage the shift themselves by endorsing something radical. But more often than not, politicians react to the window rather than moving it. The factors that move the Overton window are often complex and dynamic, not easily controlled, and often a result of a slow evolution of societal values and norms.

Media and culture play a far larger role in the movement of societal values than politicians do. However, in the modern era of social media-driven politics, that's beginning to change. Politics and the media are becoming intertwined and collaborative instead of distinct and separate. Once in the history of our nation, it was believed that the role of the media was to present an unbiased and thorough reporting of the news so the American people could be informed. However, it is now the case that the media actively engages in politics, with biases clear and present. Politicians are also now engaging in the new media. With websites like Twitter, Youtube, Facebook, and dozens of others, the internet has made politicians more accessible to people than ever before. It has also made people more accessible to politicians.

With this newfound accessibility of information and access, the media has been reshaped from a prime-time news hour and a daily print run to a 24-hour cycle of streaming news. Opinions and biases are present in all forms of alternative media, the people are more susceptible to its influence than ever before. This means that the Overton window is more susceptible to rapid movement than ever before as well. When trying to sell the public on fringe ideologies way outside the Overton window, you have to start by taking steps to move the focus of the window in the right direction, towards your policies, even if not all the way to including them.

Engaging in New Media

Make no mistake about it, the world of media has changed, and will never go back to the way it was. The exponential advancement in communications technology and web infrastructure since the advent of the public internet has been unstoppable. But this is a good thing for those of us on the fringes. Prior to the age of mass communication media, we had to rely on journalists and their ilk to cover us, give us airtime, and tell the populace that our ideas were safe enough for them to consider. But in the internet age, we have direct access to everyone we want to reach, and the ability to create our own platforms to do so.

The 2020s have seen the rise of alternative media. From Twitter journalists to Youtube talk shows, the news is no longer the province of the mainstream media and is no longer limited to its reach. Independent journalists have taken the world by storm, and politics have responded by trying to catch up to the shift in the Overton window towards more radical and fringe ideologies finding acceptance among the people. The beauty of alternative media is the accessibility it provides for anyone to create their own platform and audience, centered around whatever niche they want.

    This presents an opportunity to take your brand to people in new and exciting ways. If you lie on the fringes of the Overton window, now is your opportunity to move it. But don't do it by trying to tone down your policies to make them more appealing to a broader audience. The key is to stick to your finger perspectives, and grow your audience and reach so that you convince more and more people to agree with them. If you moderate yourself, you are moving your principles to be more in line with the Overton window, but if you move more people towards your radical thought, then eventually it becomes acceptable. But whatever you do, don't let the masses move you more towards the middle.

WHY DO I CARE

So why do I care? Why Have I spent so long putting this whole guide together, in the hopes that it will help others improve their skills as salespeople for liberty? Because for me, Liberty itself is worth selling. My freedom, my principles, and my beliefs are not mere politics for me. For me, it's a final attempt to save the world and create a life worth living. In the 33 years of my life, we've watched as The United States, the last bastion of freedom in the world becomes more and more tyrannical. With government growing at every step, and the Overton window being pushed towards totalitarianism by endless wars, poverty, and economic collapse. To me, enabling others to make a difference is a matter of self-preservation.

Why I'm a Libertarian - an Essay

Jim Bouchard, the author of *Crazy, Angry, Libertarian*, argues that there is no point in someone's life where they can so radically change to say that they've "become" a Libertarian. However, each of us goes through a series of events or circumstances that shape our opinions and worldview to accept Libertarian Philosophy. Through this growth process, it is possible, and often likely, that we will have a culminating event that does affect us in such a manner that we can suddenly come to the realization that we always were a Libertarian, and just never realized it. This is the story of my moment.

I don't often talk about my service in the Military, because as a politician and an activist I aim to have people focus on my ideas, and my policies, rather than my accomplishments and my titles. Yet when I was younger, that uniform was something I wore proudly, and a culture I embraced and exuded at every step. I grew up in a very conservative household, Joined the Army at 18, attended a regimented Military Academy for college, and was fast-tracked into a career in law enforcement. I spent my weekends in college interning at the local police department, or on assignment from the national guard, whether in operational support or emergency response. From Blizzards and Hurricanes to regular security details at public events, I proudly donned the uniform and carried out the duties I was assigned. So it should be no surprise that while most of my college friends celebrated the 4th of July with Beers and Barbecues on the Beach of Cape Cod, I spent my holiday volunteering as a member of the security detachment for the 4th of July fireworks in Boston.

But in 2013, there was something special about this event that changed everything. Just weeks earlier, I was also among the soldiers stationed in Boston to provide additional security and crowd control for the Boston Marathon. That was a Patriots day that began the reshaping of my future. After the elite runners had finished, and the crowd was at its peak with amateurs finishing their marathon, and spectators celebrating the holiday, 2 explosions ripped through the heart of Boston's proudest event, an act of terror that broke the heart, but strengthened the spirit of the city. Rather than heading home that afternoon after the marathon ended, we spent the next 2 days on high alert, with joint patrols of Military, Boston, and Massachusetts State Police officers securing the sites of the bombings and slowly coming to terms with what we had witnessed all the while ignoring the bloodstains on our boots. The people of Boston came together and rose above the tragedy, and the culture of pride drove the winds of recovery. The tragedy was short-lived before the business of life was back to normal in Boston -at least until the 4th of July.

It wasn't witnessing a terrorist attack that changed my life, and it wasn't being a party to a militarized occupation of the city of Boston for 2 days. In fact, that experience temporarily served to reinforce my cultural bias toward the need for a security state. Those experiences drove home my desire to serve and protect, and defend my home and my family from the threat of terrorism at all costs. But that only lasted a few weeks. When the call came for volunteers to serve on the security detail at the 4th of July fireworks, I was the first name on the list and made sure I would be available to do my duty.

On that particular day, there was a show of force like I had never before seen. I was the Non-Commissioned Officer in Charge of a contingent of 40 soldiers manning checkpoints on the bridges to the Boston Esplanade, and one of 10 such contingents throughout the city. There was also a strong presence from not only the Boston PD but also surrounding cities and towns who sent officers in for the details. We had TSA Agents searching bags at our checkpoints, and roving patrols of FBI, DEA, and ATF canine units mixed in throughout. for surveillance, the State Police deployed mobile camera units at every bridge crossing and ensured that no one could move freely in the area we were securing without being searched or watched. A news reporter the next day quipped in their article that it felt like there were more military and police guarding the fireworks than there were people actually enjoying them.

In the mid-afternoon, I was walking a patrol between the checkpoints, ensuring that the soldiers under my command had plenty of water, and were doing alright in the summer heat. As I turned around a corner, with my fresh Lieutenant in tow, ink not yet dried on his college degree, a man was seated in a lawn chair in the middle of our path, blocking anyone from walking past him. This alone would arouse suspicion even if it wasn't a high-alert event, but then I noticed he was reading a book. As I looked closer I could see this man sitting there in front of us, a silent form of protest, reading George Orwell's 1984, the dystopian epic about an oppressive government surveillance state depriving its citizens of freedom and privacy. As I chuckled to myself, the Lieutenant asked me what was so funny, and I just shook my head as I remarked on how we had become Big Brother.

In the name of security, and the comfort of its theater, we had stripped freedom from the very cradle of the American Revolution. Boston, the birthplace of patriots, had become succumbed to fear and capitulated to the deprivation of their own liberty. It was at that moment that I decided that I could not in good conscience reenlist in the United States Military. It was at that moment, that I came to a profound understanding of what liberty was, and how much of it we had willingly surrendered. It was at that moment, on July 4th, 2013, that I resolved to cast off my own chains of ignorance and embrace freedom at every grasp. It was at that moment, at a celebration of patriotism, that I decided to revel in its history. And it was at that moment, that I realized that I was a Libertarian...

It was that defining moment that drove me to reject the conservative teachings I had been raised on. It was that defining moment that drove me to reject the Military Culture I had embraced. It was that defining moment that drove me to change the trajectory of my entire life. I'm no longer working in or working towards a career in law enforcement, but rather endeavoring daily to end the war on drugs and stop the persecution of disparaged minorities in our country at the hands of police. I'm no longer striving for a long military service record to be proud of, but rather fighting in the trenches of public policy to end a foreign policy hell-bent on endless war and suffering around the globe.

I'm a Libertarian because I have had that moment in my life, where I came to realize that Liberty matters, that freedom is not guaranteed and that oppression can take many forms.

I'm a Libertarian because I realized someone needs to be a voice that strongly stands up to oppose gun control at every turn, but also encourages education and a chance to shift our culture away from glorifying the violence that is consuming it. I'm a Libertarian because someone needs to demand that we end the drug war, and decriminalize possession and use of all drugs- so that we can end the systemic cycle of incarceration that plagues our impoverished communities and disproportionately targets minorities. I'm a Libertarian, and I'm angry enough to be that angry voice calling for the withdrawal of all US troops from overseas, and an immediate end to conflict and war in our lifetime, because all people, not just Americans, deserve to sleep peacefully at night.

What Motivates You?

Before you start to implement what you've learned to try and sell your ideas to others. Take some time to reflect upon why it matters to you. What is your motivation? What drives you to be involved and get engaged? Why do you care?

The truth is, even the best salesman in the world needs to know their product isn't trash. They have to believe in it. They have to believe in themselves to sell it. So ask yourself, even with all you've learned, do you believe in Liberty enough to sell it to a stranger? When you figure out why start by telling your story.

www.ingramcontent.com/pod-product-compliance
Lightning Source LLC
Chambersburg PA
CBHW052256220526
45471CB00001B/358